The world begins to go crazy. You can't take your eyes off

SAIYUKI RELOAD

8

KAZUYA MINEKURA

WRENCH IT OPEN.
BREAK IT DOWN.

TELL ME WHAT YOU SEE ON THE OTHER SIDE.

SAIYUKI RELOAD 8
CONTENTS

最遊記
RELOAD
ミネクラカズヤ

Saiyuki Reload Volume 8
Created by Kazuya Minekura

Translation - Alethea & Athena Nibley
English Adaptation - Lianne Sentar
Retouch and Lettering - Star Print Brokers
Production Artist - Keila N. Ramos
Copy Editor - Jessica Chavez

Editor - Lillian Diaz-Przybyl
Digital Imaging Manager - Chris Buford
Pre-Production Supervisor - Lucas Rivera
Production Manager - Elisabeth Brizzi
Managing Editor - Vy Nguyen
Creative Director - Anne Marie Horne
Editor-in-Chief - Rob Tokar
Publisher - Mike Kiley
President and C.O.O. - John Parker
C.E.O. and Chief Creative Officer - Stu Levy

A TOKYOPOP® Manga

TOKYOPOP Inc.
5900 Wilshire Blvd. Suite 2000
Los Angeles, CA 90036

E-mail: info@TOKYOPOP.com
Come visit us online at www.TOKYOPOP.com

ISBN: 978-1-4278-0466-2

First TOKYOPOP printing: June 2008

10 9 8 7 6 5 4 3 2 1

Printed in the USA

Genjyo Sanzo –

A very brutal, worldly priest. He drinks, smokes, gambles and even carries a gun. He's looking for the sacred scripture of his late master, Koumyou Sanzo. He's egotistical, haughty and has zero sense of humor, but this handsome 23-year-old hero also has calm judgment and charisma. His favorite phrases are "Die" and "I'll kill you." His main weapons are the Maten Sutra, a handgun, and a paper fan for idiots. He's 177cm tall (approx. 5'10") and is often noted for his drooping purple eyes.

Son Goku –

The brave, cheerful Monkey King of legend; an unholy child born from the rocks where the aura of the Earth was gathered. His brain is full of thoughts of food and games. To pay for crimes he committed when he was young, he was imprisoned in the rocks for five hundred years without aging. Because of his optimistic personality, he's become the mascot character of the group; this 18-year-old of superior health is made fun of by Gojyo, yelled at by Sanzo and watched over by Hakkai. He's 162cm tall (approx. 5'4"). His main weapon is the Nyoi-Bo, a magical cudgel that can extend into a sansekkon staff.

Sha Gojyo –

Gojyo is a lecherous kappa (water youkai). His behavior might seem vulgar and rough at first glance (and it is), but to his friends, he's like a dependable older brother. He and Goku are sparring partners, he and Hakkai are best friends and he and Sanzo are bad friends (ha ha!). Sometimes his love for the ladies gets him into trouble. Because of his unusual heritage, he doesn't need a limiter to blend in with the humans. His favorite way of fighting is to use a shakujou, a staff with a crescent-shaped blade connected by a chain; it's quite messy. He's 184cm tall (approx. 6'), has scarlet hair and eyes and is a 22-year-old chain smoker.

Cho Hakkai –

A pleasant, rather absent-minded young man with a kind smile that suits him nicely. It's sometimes hard to tell whether he's serious or laughing to himself at his friends' expense. His darker side comes through from time to time in the form of a sharp, penetrating gaze, a symbol of a dark past. As he's Hakuryu's (the white dragon) owner, he gets to drive the Jeep. Because he uses kikou jutsu (Chi manipulation) in battle, his "weapon" is his smile (ha ha!). He's 22 years old, 181cm tall (approx. 5'11") and his eyes are deep green (his right eye is nearly blind). The cuffs he wears on his left ear are Youkai power limiters.

The Story So Far

Chaos has ravaged Shangri-La. During an attempt by dark forces to revive the Ox King Gyumaoh, the combination of science and youkai magic sent a Minus Wave surging through the land that drove all youkai berserk, thus causing mass violence and upsetting the peaceful balance between the races. Now it's up to four companions--the youkai Son Goku, Sha Gojyo, and Cho Hakkai, and the human Priest Genjyo Sanzo--to travel West and stop the experiment that plagues the world. It's an excellent plan...save for the fact that the four companions suffer from "teamwork issues."

While taking a break from their travels, Goku was suddenly and fatally attacked by an unseen enemy. Sanzo chased after Goku's attacker in a mindless rage, leaving the dying Goku in the hands of Hakkai and Gojyo. Unable to save him through normal means, the two removed Goku's diadem to test the regenerative powers of the "Seiten Taisei"....and were rewarded with a healed but completely berserk Goku. Even the aid of Hazel and Gat wasn't enough to stop Goku, leaving Hakkai with one choice--take off his own youkai power limiters and fight Goku head-on. The ensuing battle just barely restored Goku and Hakkai to their normal selves, but not without a price. Sanzo, unable to find Goku's attacker and noticeably absent during Goku's time of crisis, left his own team once the battle was through.

Hakkai, Gojyo, and Goku now continue their journey without their leader. Sanzo, meanwhile, has decided to travel with Hazel and Gat, as they seem to be the only connections to Goku's mysterious attacker. When the three of them stop at a human village to rest, the three youkai stop at a rival youkai village. And although everyone seems to be resting in relative peace, the tenuous balance can only last so long.

...
NYAÄÄAH!
I'M HOT. BOO.
THE FRIGGIN' COLD AT NIGHT KEEPS THROWING ME. I WAKE UP FREEZING, THEN BOOM-- BY NOON YOU CAN FRY AN EGG ON MY ASS.
Yawn.
DESERTS ARE FRIGHT-ENING PLACES.
act. 37
Even a worm-24
OH, YOU'RE FINALLY AWAKE?
I HATE TO THINK WHAT WOULD HAVE HAPPENED IF WE HADN'T BEEN RESCUED YESTERDAY.
HEY. MORNIN'.
GOOD MORNING. IS EVERYONE ALREADY AT WORK?

THEY'VE SURE AS HELL GOT STAMINA.
MY CALVES ARE STILL SORE FROM STANDING ALL DAY YESTERDAY.

HMPH!
CITY PEOPLE ARE SUCH WEAKLINGS.
...SHE CALLED YA A SISSY.
PFF!
SHE INCLUDED *YOU* IN THAT, CITY BOY!
HURRY UP AND WASH. THE WATER'S THAT WAY.
....

NAH-- MY LEGS'RE FINE.
MAYBE YOU'RE JUST OLD.
WHAT WAS THAT?!
YES, YES.
BY THE WAY...

WATER'S EXTREMELY VALUABLE OUT HERE.
IF YOU WASTE ANY, YOU'RE TOAST.

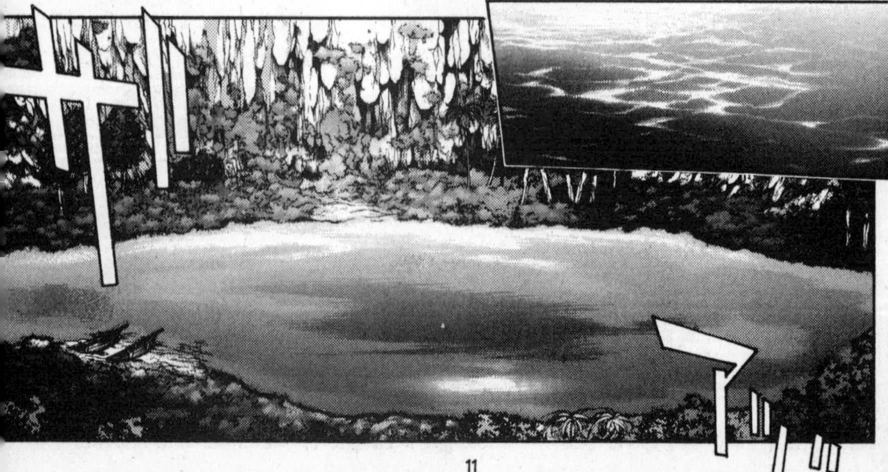

IT FEELS A BIT LIKE A RESORT HERE, DON'T IT?
WE'RE HONORED THAT YOU LIKE IT.
THE WATER OF LIFE... EH?

IT EXPLAINS WHY THIS TOWN CAN STILL THRIVE IN THE DESERT.

IN-DEED, GOOD SIR.
WE DESERT PEOPLE CAN'T LIVE AWAY FROM THIS SPRING.

HM.
AND Y'ALL SAY THERE'S A GROUP THAT'S THREATENIN' THE SPRING?

YOU'RE AS SHARP AS THE RUMORS SAY, SIR.

MY LORD BISHOP, MY LORD PRIEST... PLEASE SAVE OUR TOWN.
IT'S IN DANGER OF FALLING INTO THE VILLAINOUS HANDS OF YOUKAI.
AGH!
NEEEEEIGH!
AAAAAAH!
WAAAAH!
WHAT JUST HAP-PENED?!
WAH!
WAAAAAAH!
AAAAAH!
THE WHEEL ON A CART BROKE, AND SOME KID GOT TRAPPED UNDER THE CARGO!
QUICK-- GET IT OFF HIM!
IS HE OKAY?!

ヒョ
SUCK IT UP, KID.
BOYS DON'T CRY.

HIC ...

HAKKAI, TAKE CARE OF HIM.
ALL RIGHT.
THE WHEEL JUST...
YOUR PROBLEM'S RIGHT HERE. SEE?

THIS'LL TAKE A WHILE TO FIX.
REALLY? HM... I GUESS I'LL HAVE TO BORROW ANOTHER CART.
HEY!
WHERE D'YA WANT ME TO TAKE THIS STUFF?
EEGH!
ER, WELL ...
ALL RIGHT. TO THE MARKET, THEN.
スタスタ
スタ
oof.
YES, SIR!
THERE-- ALL BETTER?
Y-YEAH.
WOW.

THOSE ARE SOME INCREDIBLE YOUKAI POWERS YOU HAVE THERE, BOYS.
YOU'RE LIFE-SAVERS!
OH, NO.
DESPITE APPEARANCES, WE'RE REALLY MEN ON THE EDGE OF SURVIVAL.
Okay.
PULL THAT OVER THERE.
ON THREE. ONE, TWO...
OH.
....

GAAH!
IT'S HOT AS *HELL* OUT HERE!
IT'S LIKE A NATURAL SAUNA.
AN' IF WE'RE NOT IN TH' SHADE, WE CAN'T EVEN TOSS OUR SHIRTS.

......
WHISPER
BUT SOMEHOW...
BEIN' HERE LIKE THIS...IT'S AS IF OUR LIVES BEFORE WEREN'T REAL.
WE WERE ALWAYS BEATIN' OFF TH' YOUKAI THAT CAME TO FIGHT US.

IT WAS AS NORMAL AS BREATHIN'.
IT'S THE SANZO PARTY! GET 'EM!

WE'RE NOT REALLY...

HERE.
HUH? OH-- COOL!
IT WOULD BE A PAIN IF YOU FAINTED AGAIN.
BUT IS IT OKAY? I KNOW WATER'S REAL IMPORTANT AN' ALL...

DAMN, GIRL. YOU REALLY *ARE* UNCUTE.
......
YOU SAID THERE'S AN OASIS ON THE OTHER SIDE OF THAT HILL, DIDN'T YOU?
IS THAT WHERE YOU GET YOUR WATER FROM?

OF COURSE NOT. THE HUMANS OCCUPY THAT TERRITORY.
WE GET OUR WATER FROM A LOT FARTHER OUT-- BEYOND THE DESERT.

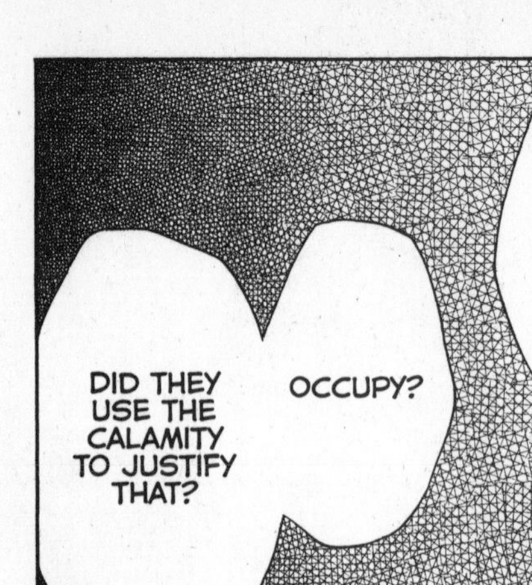
OCCUPY?
DID THEY USE THE CALAMITY TO JUSTIFY THAT?

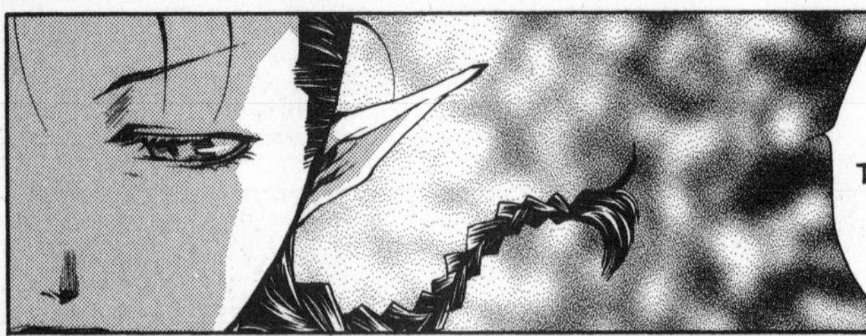
IT HAPPENED WAY BEFORE THE "CALAMITY," OR WHATEVER YOU CALL IT.

THE YOUKAI WHO USED TO LIVE AT THAT OASIS WERE CHASED OUT BY THE HUMANS.
WE STILL GOT OUR WATER FROM THERE FOR A WHILE...BUT WE'VE BEEN COMPLETELY SHUT OUT SINCE THEY THINK WE WENT CRAZY.
WHEN THE HUMANS SETTLED IN FOR GOOD, THE YOUKAI HAD NO CHOICE BUT TO SET UP A VILLAGE HERE.
THESE DAYS, THEY'RE ARMING THE TOWN LIKE A FORTRESS.

ANY YOUKAI WHO GETS CLOSE TO THAT HILL GETS SHOT AND KILLED.
EVEN THOUGH YOUKAI ARE TOUGHER'N HUMANS...
...THEY STILL CAN'T LIVE WITHOUT WATER.
...AND YOU SAY THIS STARTED BEFORE THE CALAMITY.
"REALITY'S NOT THAT SWEET--HUMANS'VE ALWAYS BEEN ON TOP."
"THOSE HIGH-AND-MIGHTY BASTARDS ARE FRICKIN' PREJUDICED, Y'KNOW?"
BUT... WAIT.
THEY KNOW THAT.
THE HUMANS JUST THINK...
...WE'RE ALL BETTER OFF DEAD.

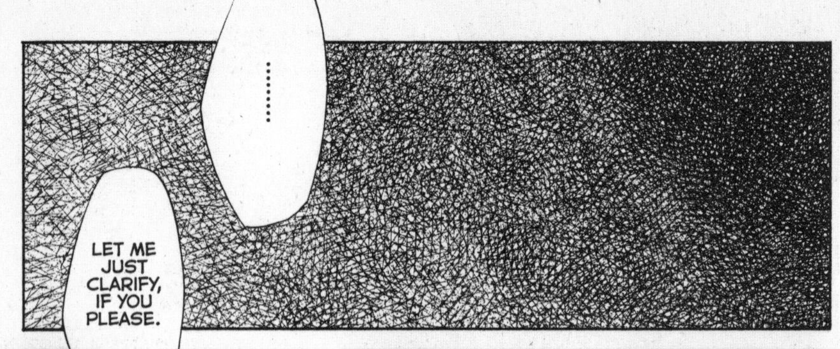
......
LET ME JUST CLARIFY, IF YOU PLEASE.

Y'ALL ARE SAYIN' THAT Y'ALL NEED THESE WEAPONS TO PROTECT THE TOWN FROM NEARBY YOUKAI?

CORRECT.
THIS TOWN HAS SUFFERED NUMEROUS DAMAGES SINCE THE YOUKAI WENT BERSERK.

THE YOUKAI HAVE BUILT A VILLAGE ON THE OTHER SIDE OF THE HILL. THEY'RE PERSISTENTLY AFTER OUR LIVES AND OUR OASIS.
CHIRP

AS YOU CAN SEE, WE'VE STRENGTH-ENED OUR ARMS IN PREPARATION FOR THEIR ATTACK...

SUCH A PITY.
WHAT IS THIS...?

BUT OUR PEOPLE STILL DON'T FEEL SAFE, SINCE THE YOUKAI COULD ATTACK AT ANY MOMENT.

SOMETHING'S NOT RIGHT HERE.
WE WOULD BE ETERNALLY GRATEFUL IF YOU MIGHT LEND US YOUR STRENGTH.

WE'RE HOPING TO ANNIHILATE THE YOUKAI VILLAGE ENTIRELY.

HEY! HAVE YOU HEARD?!
?
HEARD WHAT, GRAMPS?
THE GROUP THAT WENT OUT TO GET WATER JUST GOT BACK, AND THEY SAID...

THE RIVER'S DRIED UP?!
NOT JUST THE RIVER-- ALL THE HILLS AND FIELDS IN THE AREA ARE JUST AS BAD!

I'D HEARD THAT THE DESERTIFICATION STARTED SPREADING A LITTLE WHILE AGO, BUT...
DESERTIFICATION...IS THAT AN EFFECT OF THE CALAMITY?
WHAT'S GOING TO HAPPEN TO US?!
DAMMIT.
WITHOUT WATER, WE'LL DIE!
IF ONLY WE HAD THAT OASIS!
—?!!
YEAH... WE'D BE FINE IF WE HAD THE OASIS.
AND THAT SPRING BELONGED TO YOUKAI IN THE FIRST PLACE!
THAT'S JUST...

DAMN THOSE HUMANS!
OY.
THESE GUYS SOUND READY FOR WAR.
EVERYONE'S YOUKAI ENERGY'S RISIN'.
THIS ISN'T GOOD.
WE LEAVE 'EM ALONE, AND THEY DO NOTHIN' BUT TAKE ADVANTAGE OF US!
WE'LL GIVE 'EM A TASTE OF OUR REAL POWER!
KILL THEM!
YEAH, KILL 'EM ALL!

KILL THE HUMANS!
WAIT A SECOND!
?!!
YA CAN'T DO THAT! IT'LL SCREW TH' HUMANS *AN'* TH' YOUKAI!
GOKU.

YOU'RE... THE NEW GUYS, RIGHT?
EXCUSE ME.
I'M SURE THAT WE OUTSIDERS DON'T HAVE THE RIGHT TO INTERJECT ON THIS MATTER.

AND I APPRECIATE THAT THIS IS AN URGENT SITUATION.
BUT FROM WHAT I UNDERSTAND...
...THE HUMANS HAVE BUILT UP ENOUGH MILITARY POWER OVER THE YEARS TO FORCEFULLY KEEP YOU AWAY FROM THE OASIS.

IF YOU WERE TO GET EMOTIONAL AND MOUNT AN ATTACK NOW, THE RESULTS COULD BE FATAL.
WELL, YEAH, BUT...
ARE YOU TELLING US TO JUST SIT HERE AND DIE OF THIRST WITHOUT DOING ANYTHING?!
WE HAVE A CAR, MA'AM.

IF SOMEONE WERE WILLING TO GUIDE US, WE COULD GO AS FAR AS NEED BE TO GET YOU YOUR WATER.
...HE'S RIGHT.
AND IT'D BE A BIG HELP IF THEY DID THAT.
YEAH...
IT WILL ONLY TIDE YOU OVER IN THIS CRISIS, GRANTED, BUT WILL YOU LET US HELP THAT MUCH?
THANK YOU.
IT'S JUST... I'M SORRY TO SAY THIS AFTER WE JUST ACCEPTED YOUR HELP, MAN.

BUT YOU GUYS *ARE* OUT-SIDERS.
—!
IT'S NOT LIKE YOU'LL ALWAYS BE HERE TO GET OUR WATER FOR US.
TCH
WE'RE GONNA HAVE TO COME UP WITH AN ANSWER TO THIS OURSELVES.
IN OUR FIGHT WITH THE HUMANS.
...YES.
I THINK YOU MAY BE RIGHT IN THAT.

...“SANZO'S PARTY” ANYMORE.

SAIYUKI RELOAD

WHAT DO WE FEEL
IN THE BLUE SKY?

act. 38
Even a worm-25

SAIYUKI RELOAD

WE'RE OFF.
I THINK WE CAN BE BACK BY TOMORROW NIGHT.
BUT IF ANYTHING HAPPENS, WE'RE COUNTING ON YOU, GOKU.
RIGHT.
BE CAREFUL.
SCHK
SCHK
SCHK
"...I'M SORRY, MAN."
SCHK

"BUT YOU GUYS ARE OUTSIDERS."
......
OW!
WHAT ARE YOU DOING?
YOU MAY BE STRONG, BUT YOU SURE ARE CLUMSY.
I'VE JUST... NEVER DONE THIS KINDA THING BEFORE.
GIVE IT.
SCHKZ SCHKZ
WOOOW.
YOU'RE, LIKE, REALLY A GIRL, HUH?

WHAT'S *THAT* SUPPOSED TO MEAN?
DON'T GOT 'EM.
...I DON'T THINK.
HUNH.
I'VE JUST NEVER BEEN AROUND GIRLS BEFORE.
WHEN I LIVED WITH SANZO, IT WAS IN A TEMPLE FULL OF GUYS.
WHAT ABOUT YOUR PARENTS?
COME TO THINK OF IT...
...I GUESS SANZO'S KINDA MY FOSTER DAD.
"SANZO"?
HEY.
I'M GOIN' OUT TO GET READY FOR TOMORROW.

HEY!
IF YOU LEAVE WITH HIM, WHO'S GOING TO EAT THIS HUGE BREAKFAST?
ERK.
OH, RIGHT!
IF YA NEED ME TO HELP, I'LL COME.
NAH, HE CAN STAY.
IT'S THE USUAL STUFF--I'LL BE FINE BY MYSELF.
I'LL BE BACK BY LUNCH.
AND DON'T THINK YOU CAN TOUCH MY SISTER JUST BECAUSE YOU'RE ALONE WITH HER, PUNK.

DAH?!
Ha Ha!
GOOD LUCK, KID.
HEY.
ACK!
WH-WHAT?!

WILL YOU CARRY THIS OVER THERE FOR ME?
OH.
SURE, I CAN DO THAT!

?
WHY ARE YOU RED ALL OF A SUDDEN?
AAAAAH! IT'S N-NOTHIN', I SWEAR!
WHY'D HER BROTHER HAVE TO GO AN' SAY THAT WEIRD STUFF TO ME?
I'm not a perv like stupid Gojyo.
NOW I'M JUST GONNA WORRY ABOUT IT.

I MEAN, SERIOUSLY...
...I JUST REALIZED IT NOW.

THIS'S A FIRST FOR ME.

......
"WATER BRINGS PROSPERITY."

TO THINK A SANZO PRIEST AND A BISHOP WOULD APPEAR TOGETHER. THIS IS TRULY THE OASIS' BLESSING.

BUT I THINK WE'LL NEED SOME SORT OF TRIGGER TO GET THEM TO TAKE ACTION.

GO AND PICK OUT TWO OR THREE YOUKAI TONIGHT.
I THINK THAT SHOULD NATURALLY...

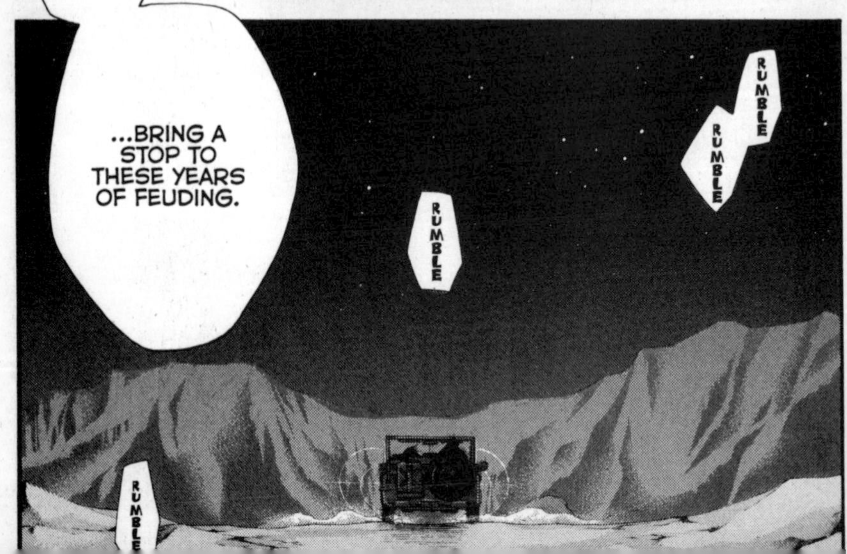
...BRING A STOP TO THESE YEARS OF FEUDING.
RUMBLE
RUMBLE
RUMBLE
RUMBLE

RUMBLE
ZZZZ
RUMBLE
RUMBLE
RUMBLE
......
YOU AWAKE?
RUMBLE
RUMBLE
I JUST CAN'T GET COMFORTABLE IN THE PASSENGER'S SEAT.
YOU WERE THE ONE WHO WANTED TO SWITCH EVERY TWO HOURS.
RUMBLE
WELL, IT DOES SEEM LIKE WE'LL BE DRIVING A WHILE.

IT'S NO USE THINKING ABOUT IT NOW-- LIFE CAN TAKE US IN ODD DIRECTIONS.
BUT WE OWE THOSE VILLAGERS THIS MUCH, AT LEAST.
......
WHAT THE HELL ARE WE DOING?
...I DON'T MEAN *THAT.*
I KNOW.
THE YOUKAI ARE SUPPOSED TO BE OUR ENEMIES.
THEY HAVE THEIR OWN WAY OF LIFE, AND THEIR OWN RACIAL THINKING.
THEY MAY NOT HAVE THE SAME FORM AS THAT OF HUMANS, BUT I WONDER IF THERE'S ANY DIFFERENCE.
STILL ...
I DON'T THINK WE CAN AFFORD TO MAKE ANY MISTAKES.

THAT ISN'T A PLACE WHERE WE BELONG.
......
RIGHT.

AAAAAAAAH!
HUH?!
NO!

IT'S ...
IT'S A YOUKAI!
NNGH...!

WH-WHAT THE HELL IS GOING ON?
HOW DID I END UP HERE?!
WHAT ARE YOU PEOPLE DOING TO ME?!
MOVE!
AAAAAH!
I'LL KILL ALL YOU DIRTY HUMANS!

BANG

ふあ
YAAAAAAWN...
ああああ.

TH' SUN WON'T QUIT GLARIN'.
AN' I COULDN'T SLEEP FOR CRAP.

FWUMP
Hmph.
IT'S NOT LIKE I FEEL *GUILTY* OR ANYTHIN'.
BUT MAYBE THAT'S WHY I...
Rrgh.

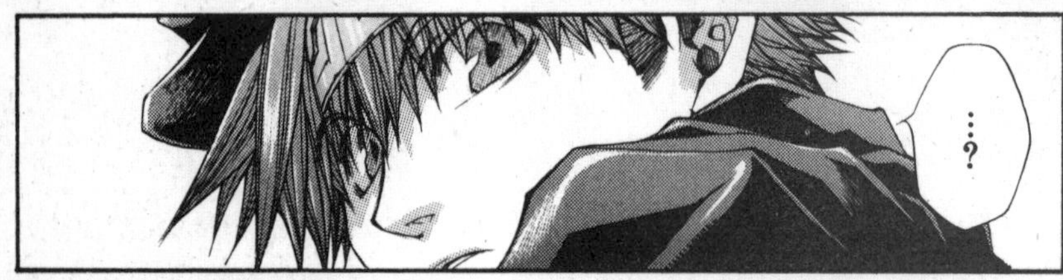
...?

.......?!
WHAT TH' HECK IS THIS?

HEY! THAT SHED OVER THERE--
?!!
!!!

AAAAAAAAAAH! I'M SORRY-- I'M REALLY, REALLY SORRY!
GAH!
DON'T OPEN THE CURTAIN WITHOUT *WARNING* ME, YOU IDIOT!

Nngh!
MAN, THIS SUCKS!
I MEAN... NOT THAT IT *SUCKS* SUCKS, BUT...
A MARK...
RIGHT.
SHE'S A YOUKAI.
WELL?
YOU WANT-ED SOME-THING?

OH.
NO, I JUST...

I SAW THAT STORAGE SHED.
THOSE'RE ALL WEAPONS, AREN'T THEY?

?
WHAT ABOUT IT?

HUH?
I THOUGHT YESTERDAY MADE IT PRETTY CLEAR THAT OUR "PEACE" IS A FAÇADE.
THE HUMANS ARE ARMED, AND WE'VE BEEN FEUDING WITH THEM.
IT WOULDN'T BE UN-EXPECTED FOR A BATTLE TO BREAK OUT AT ANY TIME.

......
WELL... I GUESS, BUT...
WHAT AM I SAYING?

THE TRUTH IS, EVERYONE'S UNEASY LIVING LIKE THIS.
YOU'RE A TRAVELER. YOU FEEL THAT, DON'T YOU?
I GUESS... I GUESS I WANNA THINK THEY'RE DIFFERENT.
I WANNA THINK TH' YOUKAI THAT LIVE HERE...
......
...AREN'T TH' SAME AS TH' YOUKAI THAT I'VE BEEN FIGHTIN'.

YOU SHOULD JUST STAY HERE.

YOU KNOW...
...THE MORE COMRADES YOU HAVE, THE BETTER.
...WAIT.
BUT...
...GOKU?
BUT I...
......!
I'M SORRY!

…………
OH!
GOOD MORNING. YOU'RE OUT EARLY TODAY.
THANKS FOR YOUR HELP YESTERDAY, KID!

I CAN'T.

I CAN'T STAY HERE.

WHAT'S THE MATTER ?
?
HEY, WHAT HAPPEN-ED?!
THIS IS BAD!
HURRY-- SOMEONE BRING A STRETCHER!

THAT'S... CRUEL.
WHO WOULD DO SOMETHIN' SO...
NO.

HE... HE SAID HE'D BE BACK FOR LUNCH.

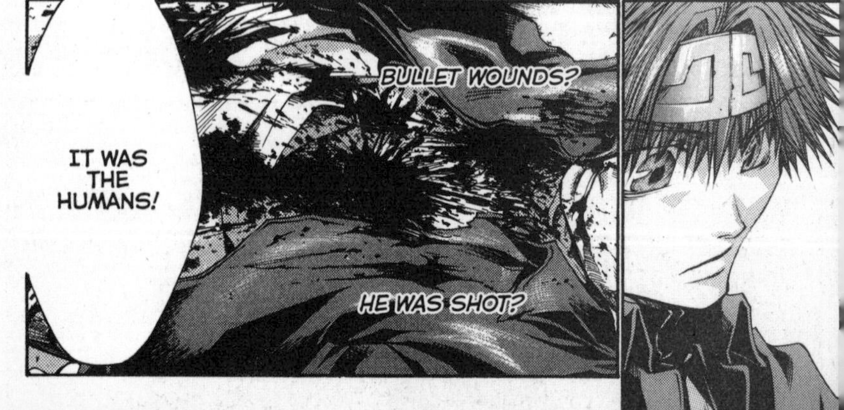
BULLET WOUNDS?
HE WAS SHOT?
IT WAS THE HUMANS!

WHO *ELSE* BUT THE HUMANS WOULD DO THIS?!
HIS BODY WAS LEFT ON THE GROUND NEAR THE HILL! THE HUMANS AT THE OASIS DID THIS!
THE FACT THAT HE WAS KILLED BY A GUN PROVES IT!
DAMMIT-- THOSE BASTARDS!
SO IT'S FINALLY COME TO THIS!
H-HANG ON!
SHUT UP!
DO YOU THINK THIS MAN WENT AFTER THE HUMANS FOR NO REASON?!
HE DIDN'T DO ANYTHING! THEY KILLED HIM FOR NOTHING!

WE CAN'T TAKE THIS ANYMORE!
FIRST THEY STEAL OUR WATER--NOW THEY WANT OUR LIVES!
WAIT A--

!!
ARE YOU OKAY?!

THIS IS WAR!

FOR OUR YOUKAI PRIDE AND AUTHORITY!
KILL THE HUMANS!
KILL ALL THE HUMANS!
......!!!

"WHAT, YOU'RE GOING OUT WITHOUT COVERING UP?"
act. 39
Even a worm-26
"YOU WON'T LAST HALF AN HOUR BEFORE GETTING HEAT-STROKE."
NEEEEIGH!

"I WORE IT WHEN I WAS A KID. IT'S PRETTY DIRTY, BUT..."
"HA! IT DOESN'T LOOK HALF BAD ON YOU."
...WHY?
WHY'D THINGS HAVE TO HAPPEN LIKE THIS?
IT WAS BOUND TO HAPPEN EVENTUALLY.

EVERYONE KNEW THIS DAY WOULD COME. THEY WERE RESIGNED TO IT, REALLY.
......
MISTER SANZO.
YOU WEREN'T IN YOUR ROOM LAST NIGHT. WHERE'D YOU RUN OFF TO?
I HEAR A YOUKAI APPEARED IN TOWN.
THAT'S RIGHT.
BUT I TOOK CARE OF THE SITUATION BEFORE THINGS GOT OUTTA HAND.
...WHAT DID HE COME INTO TOWN FOR?

I'M NOT RIGHTLY SURE. TO ATTACK THE HUMANS, I S'POSE.
ALONE?
AND I THINK IT WOULD BE PRETTY DIFFICULT JUST TO GET *INSIDE* AN ARMED TOWN.

I CAN'T HELP YOU THERE.
I JUST WENT BECAUSE I HEARD THERE WAS A YOUKAI RUNNIN' AMOK IN TOWN, IS ALL.

...IS THERE SOMETHIN' YOU'RE TRYIN' TO SAY?
HOW DISGUST-INGLY CONVEN-IENT.
MY GOAL'S TO TAKE DOWN THE YOUKAI AND SAVE THE HUMANS.
I'VE SAID THAT ALREADY.
....

"EVEN A ONE-INCH WORM HAS A HALF-INCH SOUL."
DO YOU KNOW THAT SAYING?
......?
IT MEANS THAT EVEN WORMS ARE LIVIN' CREATURES, RIGHT?
HN.
IT'S NOT LIKE YOU TO BE GIVIN' SUCH STALE SERMONS, MISTER SANZO.
YOU SHOULD GO BACK WEST AND TAKE ANOTHER LOOK AT A DICTIONARY.
EXCUSE ME?

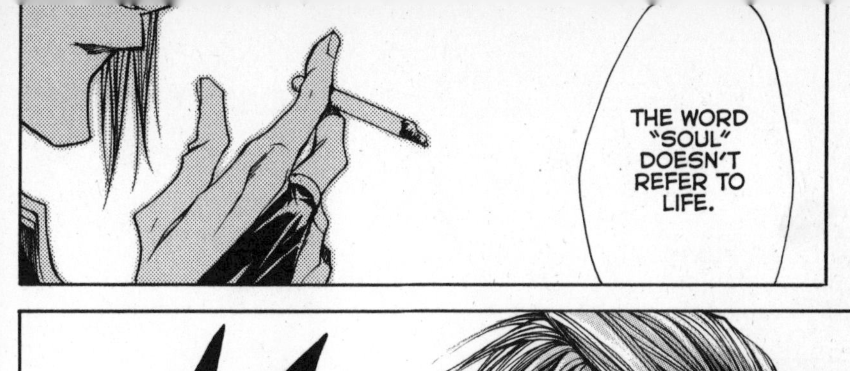
THE WORD "SOUL" DOESN'T REFER TO LIFE.

IT REFERS TO "PRIDE."

!!?
WHAT WAS THAT?!
MY LORD PRIEST! MY LORD BISHOP!

THE YOUKAI ARE ATTACKING!
WE BELIEVE THEY'RE RETALIATING FOR WHAT HAPPENED YESTERDAY.
PLEASE LEND US YOUR POWERS FOR THE SAKE OF OUR TOWN!

....
I WONDER WHAT'S GOIN' ON AT TH' OASIS RIGHT NOW.
HOW'RE TH' VILLAGERS DOIN'?
MAN...I CAN'T CALM DOWN.
AN' I CAN'T LEAVE TH' VILLAGE 'TIL GOJYO AN' HAKKAI GET BACK.

AN' I KINDA FELT LIKE I SHOULDN'T STOP 'EM.
BUT...
...I COULDN'T STOP 'EM.

WHY CAN'T I DO ANYTHIN'?!
CRAP!
GOKU.
THIS IS ALL OF THEM.
...UH, RIGHT.

HEY! YOU'RE HUNGRY, RIGHT?
WE'VE GOT SOME FOOD FOR YA.

......
NOW I'M LYIN'.
CHEER UP, KID!
THIS'S BAD.
YOUR MOM AN' DAD'LL BE BACK IN NO TIME!
OKAY?

A LONG TIME AGO...
...I'D GET REALLY WORRIED WHENEVER SANZO WOULD LEAVE ME, TOO.
MAN.
WHAT WOULD SANZO SAY IF HE WAS HERE?

WHAT WOULD SANZO--

DON'T HURT YOURSELF TRYING SO HARD.

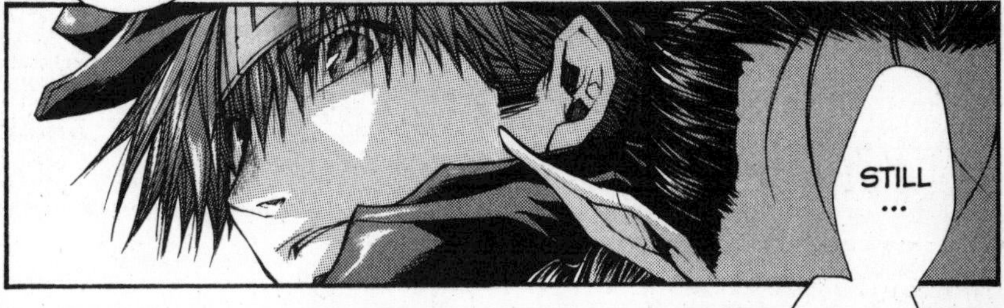
STILL ...

THANK YOU.

YAAAAAAH!
?!!

EEEEK!
THE HUMANS ARE COM--
HAGH!
......!!
AM I CLEAR ?!

DON'T LEAVE A SINGLE YOUKAI ALIVE!
NOW THAT THE VILLAGE IS ALMOST EMPTY, WE CAN ERADICATE THE YOUKAI ONCE AND FOR ALL!
......
THOSE DIRTY...!

GAGH!
GGHCK!
......?!
HGH!

YOU ROTTEN, PATHETIC LITTLE HUMANS!
DON'T YOU DARE TRY AND DEFY US YOUKAI!
...WHAT IS THIS?
GUGH!
DISGUSTING... BEASTS!

I...
WHAT ARE YOU JUST STANDING THERE FOR?!
THIS WAY!

WHAT'M I FIGHTIN'?
HAA ...
HAA ...
DAMMIT.
HOW DID THEY KNOW THE VILLAGE IS ALMOST EMPTY?
OUR MILITIA SHOULD ONLY BE GETTING THERE NOW!

IT WAS A TRAP.
HUH?

I THINK THEY JUST... TRICKED EVERYONE IN TH' VILLAGE INTO ATTACKIN' TH' OASIS.
THEY DID THAT STUFF TO YOUR BROTHER TO GET TH' YOUKAI RILED UP.
.........!!

DAMMIT!
DAMMIT!
THOSE SONS OF... HUMANS!
DAMMIT...
STOPPIT.

WHOSE SIDE ARE YOU ON, GOKU?!

HAAAAAGH!
GGGGGH!
GAGH!
YAAAAH!
ALL OF OUR TROOPS WERE STATIONED AT THE NORTH GATE OF THE MOUNTAIN, SO WE HAVE THE ADVANTAGE.
BUT WE CAN'T LET OUR HUBRIS DISTRACT US. WE'RE UP AGAINST YOUKAI-- *MONSTERS.*
I WOULD STILL BE GRATEFUL IF THE THREE OF YOU USED YOUR POWERS TO ANNIHILATE THEM.

...IT'S ALWAYS GOOD TO LAY THE GROUND-WORK.
I ASSUME YOU'VE ALREADY GONE AFTER THE YOUKAI VILLAGE.
...?!
HOW...
PARDON ME?

WELL, WELL. THE FINEST PRIEST IN SHANGRI-LA IS AS INTELLIGENT AS I WOULD HAVE HOPED.
BUT WE'VE *ALWAYS* BEEN PREPARED FOR THIS TURN OF EVENTS, LORD PRIEST.
IT'S THE FRUIT OF OUR DAILY TRAINING.
YOU MAY HAVE ARMED THIS TOWN WITH YOUR FETISH FOR FIREPOWER...

...BUT YOU DIDN'T SOUNDPROOF THIS BUILDING.
I HAD TO LISTEN TO YOUR "SECRET" CONVERSATIONS WHETHER I WANTED TO OR NOT.

WHATEVER ARE YOU TALKING ABOUT?
I WALKED AROUND TOWN, BUT I DIDN'T SEE ANY SIGNS OF DAMAGE.
THIS IS NOTHING BUT A PEACEFUL, BEAUTIFUL OASIS.
......?
FROM THE VERY BEGINNING, SOMETHING SEEMED OFF HERE.
YOU WEREN'T SCARED ENOUGH TO HAVE BEEN ATTACKED BY YOUKAI AS OFTEN AS YOU CLAIMED.

THE ONLY THING THAT MUDDIES IT...
...IS THAT YOU'RE ALL SO DIRTY AS TO STEAL THE YOUKAI'S WATER *AND* THEIR LIVES.

......?!

......
CRAP.
WHAT AM I DOIN'?

I'M... SORRY ABOUT EARLIER.

"WHOSE SIDE ARE YOU ON, GOKU?!"
WHAT-EVER.
IT'S, UH, OKAY.

I'M TH' ONE THAT'S SORRY.
YOU? WHY SHOULD *YOU* APOLOGIZE?

'CAUSE I CAN'T... DO ANYTHIN'.
...THE WANTED MEN.
"PRIEST SANZO AND HIS PARTY."

Ha Ha!
SO YOU GUYS REALLY *ARE* THEM.
HOW'D YOU...?

I TOLD YOU, DIDN'T I? I'M A FAN OF LORD KOUGAIJI'S.
LORD KOUGAIJI'S ARCH-NEMESIS PRIEST SANZO HAS THREE YOUKAI SERVANTS TRAVELING WITH HIM. EVEN I KNOW *THAT* MUCH.
OH, CRUD. WHAT'D I SAY YESTER-DAY?

"I GUESS SANZO'S KINDA MY FOSTER DAD."
BUT WHATEVER.

IT'S NOT LIKE IT REALLY CHANGES MY OPINION OF YOU.
YOUR TYPE'S NOT SHARP ENOUGH TO LIE, ANYWAY.
OW.

HAVE YOU ALWAYS BEEN TRAVELING IN THAT CAR?
WHAT'S IT LIKE IN THE EAST?

OH.
WELL, TH' WEATHER'S WAY DIFFERENT FROM HERE.
IT RAINS A LOT, AN' IT SNOWS SOMETIMES.
SNOW, HUH? I'VE NEVER SEEN ANYTHING OTHER THAN DESERT.
THERE'RE MOUNTAINS THAT'RE GREEN ALL OVER.
BUT WHEN YA GO TO BIG TOWNS, THEY'RE FULLA SHOPS AN' STUFF.

AN' THERE'S TONS OF AWESOME FOOD!
WHAT IS IT WITH YOU AND FOOD?!
C'MON-- FOOD'S TH' BEST PART OF TRAVELIN'!

...HM.
KOFF!
I'VE ALWAYS WANTED TO GO SEE THAT.
KOFF!
KOFF!
WHAT'S THE MAT-TER?

IT KINDA SMELLS LIKE SMOKE.
BUT WHY?
IT DOES SEEM HOTTER IN HERE.
AND THE SUN'S ALREADY SET.
!!
GOKU!

......
OUR VILLAGE...
BURN IT DOWN!

BURN IT TO THE GROUND-- DON'T EVEN LEAVE A WORM!
YES, SIR!
?!!
WHA--

LET GO, YOU LITTLE BRAT! ARE YOU ANOTHER DIRTY YOUKAI?!
STOPPIT.
!!? I CAN'T... MOVE IT!
HOW CAN HE BE THAT STRONG?!
YOU!
MONSTER!

AAGH!
GAAH!

WHAT THE *HELL?!*
THERE'S STILL MORE FRIGGIN' YOUKAI!
AAAAAAAAAH!

GOKU...
IT'S NOT ABOUT HUMAN OR YOUKAI.
OR WHOSE SIDE I'M ON.
THIS'S ABOUT WHAT'S IMPORTANT TO *ME*.

SO Y'ALL TRICKED ME INTO THIS?

"TRICK" IS SUCH A STRONG WORD.
WE ONLY HAD YOU GIVE THE YOUKAI A REASON TO ACT.

BY HAVING HAZEL TAKE CARE OF THE YOUKAI YOU BROUGHT HERE?

THE YOUKAI ARE THE ONES WHO ARBITRARILY WAGED THIS WAR.
WE'RE THE VICTIMS HERE.
AND WE WEREN'T THE ONES WHO LIT THE FUSE, LORD BISHOP.
YOU DID THAT FOR US.
......!!
HOOK, LINE AND SINKER.

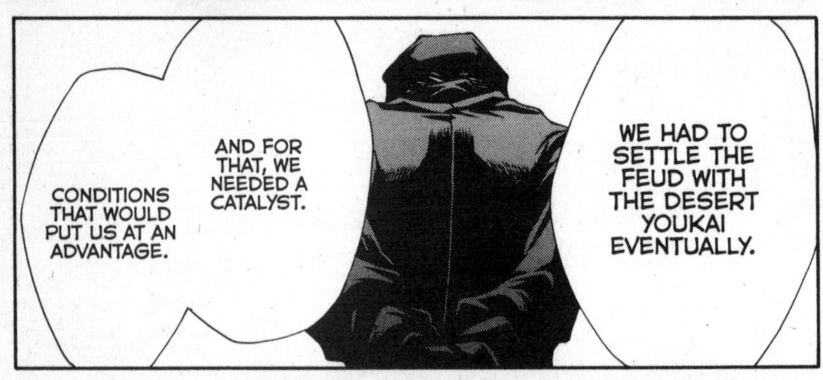
WE HAD TO SETTLE THE FEUD WITH THE DESERT YOUKAI EVENTUALLY.
AND FOR THAT, WE NEEDED A CATALYST.
CONDITIONS THAT WOULD PUT US AT AN ADVANTAGE.

WELL, I'LL BE.
IN ORDER TO KEEP YOUR OWN HANDS CLEAN, Y'ALL TRICKED US INTO THINKIN' THAT REMOVIN' THE YOUKAI WAS A JUST CAUSE.

I'M SURE YOU UNDERSTAND.
BISHOP HAZEL GROSSE, WHO STEALS YOUKAI LIVES IN ORDER TO REVIVE HUMANS.
VICIOUS, BRUTAL YOUKAI WERE NEVER MEANT TO COEXIST WITH HUMANS.
FOR THE PEACE OF THE HUMANS IN SHANGRI-LA--NO, FOR HUMANS ALL OVER THE WORLD, WE MUST ERADICATE THE YOUKAI.
NOT THAT I MEAN THAT AS A CRITICISM.
YOUR VIEWS ARE OUR IDEAL, LORD BISHOP. IT'S PRECISELY YOUR POWER...

...THAT WE HOLD UP AS OUR HOPE.
ギー
ギーイ...

NOW, MY LORD.

PLEASE GRANT US THE POWER OF HOPE.
FOR THE SAKE OF ALL HUMANS.

SHOULDN'T WE BE GETTING THERE SOON?
WE *ARE* GETTING BACK A BIT LATE, AREN'T WE?

—?
WHAT'S THAT?
WHAT'S WHAT?

WAIT... WHY'S THAT AREA ALL RED?
IT... CAN'T BE.

!!!
IT'S FIRE!
AND IT'S COMING FROM THE VILLAGE!
WHAT?!
HOLD ON TO SOMETHING, BOTH OF YOU!
KK-CHCK

Lay your voiceless shout on the dissipating white smoke.
act. 40
Even a worm-27

SAIYUKI RELOAD

CRAP! I CAN'T--
GRAND-MA!
GRAND-MA, HANG ON!
——!!
NNGH...
L-LEAVE ME.
YOU HAVE TO... RUN!
........!!

BUT REMEMBER THIS, CHILD.
YOU MUST NEVER, EVER...
...REGRET THAT YOU WERE BORN A YOUKAI.
GRANDMA?
GRAND-MA!
WAAAAAAH!
WAAAAAAH!
......

HOW... HORRIBLE!
HOW COULD THEY DO THIS TO THE VILLAGE?!

YOU'RE BACK?! WHAT HAPPENED TO EVERYBODY ELSE?!
HOW'S THE BATTLE GOING?!
THE HUMANS HAVE US COMPLETELY OUTNUM-BERED IN ARMS AND TROOPS.
I CAME TO GET WEAPONS AND REINFORCE-MENTS, BUT...

...SORRY.
THERE'S NOTHING LEFT HERE.
DAMMIT!
WE WERE SO CLOSE...!

WAIT.
IF YOU WANT GUN POWDER...
...THERE'S STILL SOME LEFT IN THE UNDERGROUND WAREHOUSE.
......!!

WHERE IS IT?
FOLLOW ME.
GOKU.
TAKE THE KIDS TO A SAFE, OPEN PLACE.

UH... RIGHT.
Waaaaah!
Waaaaah!
NO!
NO, WE WANNA STAY HERE!
EVERY-ONE'S GONNA DIE ANYWAY!
EVEN US!
NO.

DIDN'T YA HEAR YOUR GRAMMA?
SHE TOLD YA NOT TO BE SAD.
THAT MEANS... IT'S OKAY FOR YA TO LIVE.

EVEN IF PEOPLE SAY YOU'RE MONSTERS.
EVEN IF YOU DON'T REALLY KNOW WHO YA ARE, EITHER.
"IT MEANS I'LL ONLY USE MY POWER 'TIL YOUKAI ARE WIPED CLEAN OFF THE FACE OF THE WORLD."

EVEN THEN.

IT'S STILL OKAY TO LIVE.

WAIT!
--!!
WHAT'S WRONG WITH YOU?! WE'LL BE FINE, JUST GO BACK, YOU STUPID--!
WHO'RE YOU...
...CALLIN' STUPID, STUPID ?!

...!
WHAT ARE YOU DOING?!
WHY'RE YA GOIN' WITH THIS GUY?!
WHY ARE YOU DOING THIS, GOKU?
STOP IT.
YOU KNOW THE ANSWER TO THAT.
......

TH-THERE'S TONS OF FUN STUFF WAITIN' FOR YA AFTER THIS.
YA CAN SEE TH' SNOW... AS MUCH AS YA WANT.
GOKU.

THIS IS HOW I CHOOSE TO LIVE.

WE HAVE OUR PRIDE.
THE ONE PERSON IN MY FAMILY, THE VILLAGE I GREW UP IN...

WHEN EVERYTHING IMPORTANT TO ME'S BEEN TAKEN AWAY, I CAN'T JUST SIT AND TAKE IT.
EVEN IF IT *IS* STUPID...
I WANT TO LIVE IN A WAY I CAN BE PROUD OF.
...I'M SURE YOU CAN UNDERSTAND THAT.
NO. NO!
I DON'T WANNA UNDER-STAND!

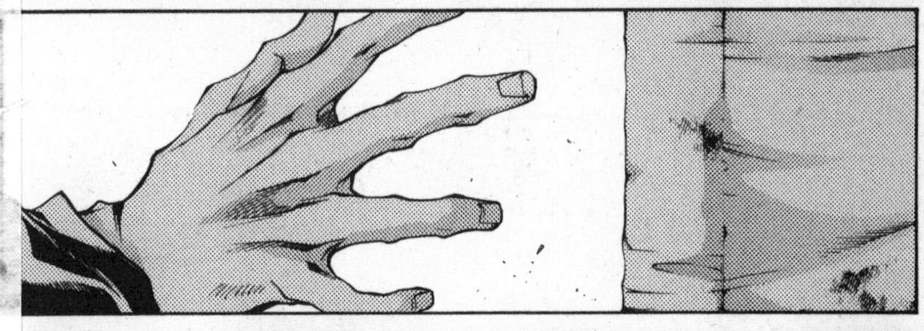

ガラ
ガラ

キキッ!!
GOKU!
HEY, ARE YOU OKAY?
WE KNOW WHAT HAPPENED.
WE JUST HEARD FROM THE CHILDREN.

WHAT CAN WE DO?

......
...UHN.

NN.
GHHCK!
....
NNGH!

...SHE WOULD'VE GROWN UP GORGEOUS.

YOUR TASTE IS A LITTLE *TOO* GOOD, KID.

MY LORD...
PLEASE GRANT US THE POWER OF HOPE.

FOR THE SAKE OF ALL WHO CALL THEMSELVES HUMAN.

I'M STARTING TO WONDER IF *THIS* IS WHY YOU MANIPULATED HAZEL.
HE TRIGGERS THE CONFLICT, WHICH FORCES HIM INTO A CORNER WHERE HE HAS TO COOPERATE ...
YOU'VE GOT PLANNING SKILLS, I'LL GIVE YOU THAT.

A CORNER?
BUT IT'S THE HONORABLE BISHOP'S JOB TO USE HIS POWER FOR HUMANS.
HE UNDERSTANDS MORE THAN ANYONE THAT YOUKAI DON'T DESERVE TO LIVE.
WELL, NOW.
YOU'RE PREACHIN' TO THE CHOIR HERE, SIR, AND YET I'M TAKIN' GREAT OFFENSE.

BUT DON'T BE MISUNDER-STANDIN' ME, MISTER SANZO. I'M NOT SYMPATHIZIN' WITH THE YOUKAI.
I JUST DON'T LIKE BEIN' TRICKED FOR *ANY* DOGGONE REASON.
I FIGURED AS MUCH.

STILL.
MERCY ME.
I SUPPOSE THERE'S NO HELPIN' IT.
I SOWED THESE SEEDS, SURE ENOUGH.

HM?
WHAT IS IT?
IF YOU DON'T AGREE WITH IT, THERE'S NO NEED TO DO IT.
—?!!

?!!
WHAT THE HELL ARE YOU--
NOW WE'VE PAID OUR DEBT.
BUT...

...THE DEBT *YOU* OWE IS EVEN GREATER.
SIR, THE YOUKAI!
THEY'VE INVADED THE FOR-TRESS!

WHAT?!
ARE YOU REALLY GOING TO ABANDON US AT A TIME LIKE THIS?!
HURRY AND ASSEMBLE ALL THE TROOPS!
THEY'RE JUST WORTHLESS YOUKAI! WHY SHOULD WE HUMANS HAVE TO GIVE A DAMN ABOUT THEIR LIVES?!
... THANKS FOR HAVING US.
PLEASE.

IF YOU HAD EVEN HALF THEIR PRIDE...
...MAYBE YOU'D UNDERSTAND.

ARE YOU SURE ABOUT THIS?
THERE ARE SO FEW OF YOU--IT'S REALLY NO TROUBLE TO TAKE YOU TO A NEARBY VILLAGE.

THANKS, BUT NO. WE CAN'T JUST LEAVE THIS PLACE LIKE THIS.
AND WE CAN'T TROUBLE YOU BOYS ANY MORE.

...WE UNDERSTAND.
AT ANY RATE, TAKE CARE.

RUMBLE RUMBLE
WHEN PUSH COMES TO SHOVE...
RUMB

...EVEN AMONG YOUKAI, WE *STILL* DON'T FRIGGIN' BELONG.
SO IT WOULD SEEM.

WE CAN'T BE HUMAN, WE CAN'T BE YOUKAI. YADDA YADDA YADDA.

WHAT-EVER.
PERHAPS...
...THERE REALLY IS NO PLACE FOR US IN THIS WORLD.
IT MAKES ME WONDER.
PERHAPS THAT'S EXACTLY WHY WE'VE BEEN ABLE TO KEEP TRAVELING LIKE THIS.

....

...L- LET'S JUST GO.
LET'S GO WEST.

UP 'TIL NOW...
SANZO WAS GOIN' WEST, AN' I WAS JUST GOIN' ALONG WITH HIM.
I WASN'T REALLY THINKIN' ABOUT IT.
WE'RE GONNA GO STOP TH' REVIVAL, RIGHT?
AN' I DON'T KNOW WHAT'S GONNA HAPPEN AFTER THAT. BUT...

BUT NOW I'M GOIN' BECAUSE I *WANNA*.
....
INDEED.

STILL ...
IF WE'RE GOING TO DO THAT, WE'LL HAVE TO PICK UP OUR LEADER FIRST, WON'T WE?
OH, YEAH.
WHY DON'T WE JUST GET WEST BEFORE SANZO CAN?
HA HA.
ADMITTEDLY, THAT MIGHT BE INTERESTING, TOO.

"DESTINY ISN'T SOMETHING THAT'S CHOSEN OR PREORDAINED."
"IT'S SOMETHING THAT ONLY BECOMES REALITY WHEN YOU FIND IT FOR YOURSELF."
NOW I UNDERSTAND WHAT HE MEANT BY THOSE WORDS.

...THIS IS MY DESTINY.

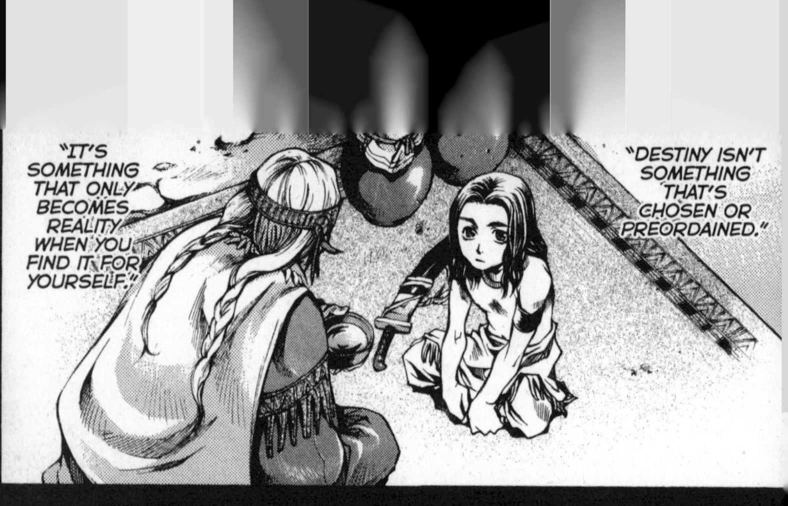

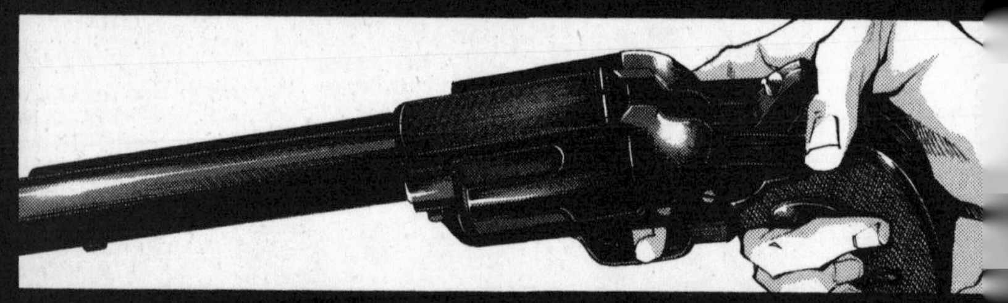

act. 41
Even a worm-28

GAH!
YAAGH!
THEY'RE ENEMIES TO YOUKAI!
KILL THEM!

OVER THERE!
CORNER HIM!

!!!!
The Father and I
are one.

HN.
I DIDN'T KNOW YOU COULD USE TECH-NIQUES LIKE THAT.
I AM AN EXORCIST, AFTER ALL.
SINCE I DON'T NEED TO COLLECT SOULS ANYMORE...
I THOUGHT I'D GET SOME EXERCISE.
REALLY.

HOW ADMIRABLE OF YOU.

HAZEL!

KOFF
KOFF
KOFF
--!
GAT!
HYA HA HA!
SO MUCH FOR YOUR GIANT!

GACK.

......
ARE YOU ALL RIGHT?

YOU GARGAN-TUAN FOOL!
IF YOU'RE PLANNIN' TO DIE, DO IT *AFTER* YOU KILL SOME-ONE!

......
I'M SORRY.

THIS SURELY IS INCONVENIENT.
BE EXTRA CAREFUL.

IF I WERE TO LOSE YOU...
...I'D BE EVEN *MORE* PUT OUT.

KAW
KAW
KAW

WHERE ARE YOU?

THAT ATTACK...
...WAS DEFINITELY INTENDED TO PROVOKE ME.

NO.
ACTUALLY...
THAT MAN'S BEEN UNDETECTABLY TOYING WITH US IN SOME FORM OR ANOTHER FOR AGES.

EVEN NOW...
...HE'S PROBABLY WATCHING US FROM SOMEWHERE AND LAUGHING TO HIMSELF.
...GET THE FUCK OUT HERE.
CRACK
KAW

KAW
KAW
KAW

... SORRY.
I THOUGHT I SENSED BLOODLUST, BUT I GUESS IT WAS JUST YOU.
HN.
YOU'VE ALWAYS MADE THE PERFECT BODY-GUARD.
....
BUT NOT FOR MUCH LONGER.

NOW THAT WE'VE LOST THAT PENDANT...
...THERE WILL EVENTUALLY BE A LIMIT TO HOW MANY TIMES I CAN BE REVIVED.
I DON'T REGRET THAT. IT'S A LIFE I'VE ALREADY LOST.
BUT...
...LOSING HIS SHIELD WILL PUT HIM AT A DISADVANTAGE.

TAKE CARE OF HAZEL.

WHAT ARE YOU TRYING TO SAY TO ME?

I KNOW YOU HAVE YOUR OWN REASONS FOR COMING WITH US.
AND I HAVE NO RIGHT TO ASK FAVORS OF YOU.
Huff
YOU'RE DAMN RIGHT YOU DON'T.

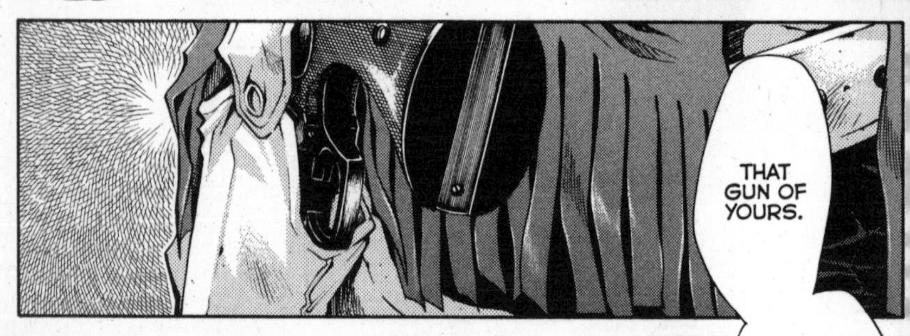
THAT GUN OF YOURS.

IT'S RIDICULOUSLY POWERFUL.
IF I TRIED TO SHOOT IT, MY ARM WOULD GO NUMB FROM THE RECOIL.

OH.
BE REAL-ISTIC.

THAT'S A GUN ONLY *YOU* CAN USE.

MEANWHILE...

I ALREADY TOLD YA!
HE'S A MUSCLEY GUY THAT'S THIIIIIIIIIIS BIG!
AND A GLARING GUY WITH EYES THIIIIIIS DROOPY.
THEY'RE WITH A NARCISSIST WHO SPEAKS IN AN AWFUL WESTERN ACCENT.
HAVE YOU SEEN THEM?
ER...

THE MOON WASN'T THE
ONLY ONE WATCHING.

act. xx
petit burial

SAIYUKI RELOAD

OWWW!
IT'S ALL... TANGLED UP AN' STUFF! I CAN'T GET IT UNDONE!
IF IT'S ALWAYS IN THE WAY, WHY DON'T YOU JUST CUT THE DAMN STUFF OFF?
?
WHY NOT?
......
I DON'T WANNA.
BECAUSE!
"IT WAS WATCHED...
...BY THE MOON ALONE."

Two years ago--Keiun Temp
WELL?
I KNOW YOU KNOW WHY I CALLED YOU HERE.
......
......
umm...

WE'RE ALL GONNA GO OUT TO EAT OR SOMETHIN'?
YOU'RE GONNA INTRODUCE ME TO A CHICK?
OF COURSE NOT, YOU SUTTOKO-DOKKOI!
ALTHOUGH "SUTTOKODOKKOI" IS A SHINTO WORD, RELATING TO SACRED MUSIC.
useless trivia.
YOU KNOW THEY DID SOME MAJOR CLEANING HERE AT KEIUN TEMPLE LAST WEEK, RIGHT?
AND WHAT DID YOU TWO DO IN THE TREASURY?
OH.
YES. GOJYO AND I WERE ROPED INTO HELPING, ACTUALLY.
HII-YA!
TAAAH!

DERYAAAAH!
I'VE OVER *HERE,* LITTLE MONKEY. MAN, DO YOU SUCK.
DON'T CALL ME MONKEY!
OOPS!
WHOA!

!!
AAGH!

...WHAT THE HELL WAS THAT?
YaaH!
CRAP-- WE BROKE IT!
...BUT NO HARM DONE.
WE PUT IT BACK TO-GETHER. SEE?
YEAH. SEE?
THAT'S NOT THE ISSUE, DAMMIT!
NO FAIR! DON'T MAKE IT MY FAULT, CRAPHEAD!
AREN'T YOU A BIT OLD TO BE DOING THESE THINGS, GOJYO?
HEY-- THAT'S ENOUGH OUTTA YOU!
I WAS JUST PLAYING WITH THE KID, ALL RIGHT?

GOJYO CAME AT ME FIRST!
ONLY BECAUSE A CERTAIN *CHIMP* WOULDN'T STOP WHINING ABOUT THE CLEANING.
STOP CALLING ME MONKEY! YOU LECHY LECHY LECHY LECHY LECHY KAPPA!
YOU WANNA PIECE OF ME, APE?!
BITE ME!
PLEASE.
LET'S TAKE A MOMENT HERE.
HUH?

WHAT TH' HECK?
WHAT'S THIS THING?
WHERE'D THEY COME FROM?
I KNEW IT.
YOU *DO* HAVE THEM.
HAVE WHAT?
THOSE ITEMS WERE "TREASURES" SEALED INSIDE THE JAR.
ARE THEY... WEAPONS, THEN?
HM.
Cheat sheet
THEY'RE SUPPOSED TO BE POSSESSED WITH DEMON POWER. THIS TEMPLE WAS KEEPING THEM SO THEY WOULDN'T BE USED FOR EVIL.
GOKU'S IS THE "NYOI-BO," WHICH CAN CHANGE SHAPE AT THE USER'S WILL, AND THE "SHAKUGET-SUJOU" CAN FREELY CONTROL A SICKLE AND CHAIN.

HOW IS THIS *STICK* A SICKLE AND CHAIN?
WAGH!

ARE YOU *TRYING* TO MAKE SASHIMI OUT OF US?!
MY BAD.
RATTLE
SO IT *IS* A SICKLE AND CHAIN.
AAAAA-AAAH! MY HAIR!
IT LOOKS LIKE HE SLICED IT OFF.
SHALL I EVEN IT UP FOR YOU LATER?
WHO CARES? IT'S JUST HAIR.
IT'LL GROW BACK.
SNAP!

YA STUPID BUTT GOBLIN!
IT WON'T GROW JUST 'CAUSE I *TELL* IT TO GROW, DUH!
....
IT GREW.
YOU TWO.
YOU DO REALIZE *WHOSE ROOM THIS IS.*
...SORRY.

WELL WHATEV I JUS HAVE GIVE T BACK RIGHT
I DON'T E REMEM TAKIN
FOR YOUR INFORMATION...
...ONCE THOSE HAVE TAKEN A MASTER, THEY STAY WITH HIM UNTIL HE DIES.
IN OTHER WORDS, YOU CAN EITHER DIE RIGHT NOW AND PUT THOSE BACK IN THE TREASURY...
...OR YOU CAN LEARN HOW TO USE THEM. IT'S YOUR CHOICE.
REALLY?
WHICH MEANS YOUR *CRASH COURSE TRAINING* STARTS TODAY. ♡
GOOD LUCK, YOU TWO!

WHAT IS IT WITH YOU AND CRASH COURSES, HAKKAI?
wait.
BEFORE YOU START ANY TRAINING, FIX MY ROOM.
FOR REAL?! FOR REAL?!
THIS IS MINE?! I CAN HAVE IT?!
OR ELSE THOSE WEAPONS ARE GOING BACK VIA OPTION A.
MY HEAD FEELS ALL... LIGHT AN' STUFF NOW.
WEIRD.
MOST PEOPLE WOULD CONSIDER THAT A GOOD THING.
MMM ...
WHY DID YOU HATE THE IDEA OF CUTTING IT, ANY-WAY?

WHEN IT GOT REALLY COLD IN THAT CAGE I WAS IN...
...IF I SPREAD OUT MY HAIR, IT FELT A LITTLE WARMER.
...'CAUSE IT WAS WARM.
WE HAVE PASTS THAT WE'VE BURIED.

HUNH. LOOKIT THE MOON.
I GUESS YOU CAN SEE IT IN THE DAYTIME, TOO.

WHAT?
HEH.
SHARP AS A TACK, AIN'T I? OF COURSE YOU CAN SEE IT DURING THE DAY.
...PERHAPS WE'VE EVEN FORGOTTEN...
...THE MOST OBVIOUS OF THINGS.
OUR BACKS TO THE MOONLIGHT...
...WE BURIED OUR BITTER "MEMORIES" DEEP IN THE NIGHT.

INSIDE THE INESCAPABLE DARKNESS.
......
ARE YOU COLD NOW?
EVEN SO.

LIKE THE MOON LEFT BEHIND IN THE BLUE SKY.
WE COME TO A REALIZATION AND LOOK TO THE HEAVENS. AND WHEN THOSE TIMES COME...
MM.
NOT REALLY.
...WE'LL CALL THEM "KEEPSAKES."

STAFF

original works

KAZUYA MINEKURA

assistant works

ASATO ASAHINA

IKUMI KATAGIRI

TAKANO

RIE TAHARA

TOMOMI NISHIYAMA

editor

YOUSUKE SUGINO

WHO?
SAIYUKI RELOAD

IT WAS A DARK AND STORMY NIGHT.
IT BEGAN IN AN OLD MANOR THAT STOOD ATOP A LONELY MOUNTAIN.
EXCUSE ME?
WE'RE FROM THE WILD BIRD RESEARCH GROUP AT ARAISO UNIVERSITY.
I'M AFRAID WE'VE LOST OUR WAY...MAY WE SPEND THE NIGHT HERE TO STAY OUT OF THE RAIN?
VERY POPULAR MYSTERY COMIC ABOUT THE VERY FAMOUS DETECTIVE HIGH PRIEST WHO WAS STILL IN COLLEGE, GENJYO SANZO. ALSO, HIS COMPANIONS.
act.xx
The Murder at Rikubousei Manor
~ Why not just bring him back to life? ~
THIS IS WHY I DIDN'T WANNA BE IN TH' WILD BIRD GROUP!
ACHOO!
IF YOU'VE GOT A PROBLEM, TELL IT TO HAKKAI.
↑ PEOPLE WHO WERE TRICKED INTO JOINING.
(BUTLER) JIKAKU.
THAT IS UNFORTUNATE.
COME THIS WAY AND SAY HELLO TO THE YOUNG MASTER OF THIS MANOR.

Y'ALL MAKE YOURSELVES AT HOME UNTIL THE STORM LETS UP, Y'HEAR?
FATHER'S ALREADY GONE TO BED, SO I'LL EXPLAIN THINGS TO HIM IN THE MORNING.
(BODYGUARD) GAT.
I WAS JUST STARTIN' TO GET BORED IN A PLACE THIS REMOTE, ANYWAY.
(HEIR TO THE ESTATE) HAZEL GROSSE.

DUDE, THIS PLACE IS *HUGE.*
AN' IT'S ALL OLD AN' COLD. IT FEELS KINDA LIKE IT'S HAUNTED.

INDEED. THERE'S AN OLD SAYIN'...
...THAT THE MASTERS OF THIS HOUSE HAVE BEEN *CURSED* FOR GENERATIONS.
CURSED?!
NOT AGAIN, YOUNG MASTER.

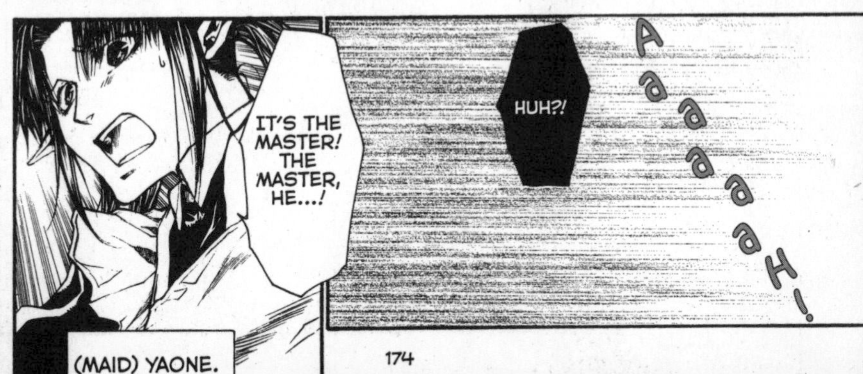
AAAAAAAH!
HUH?!
IT'S THE MASTER! THE MASTER, HE...!
(MAID) YAONE.

FATHER!
MASTER!
(MASTER OF THE ESTATE) GOUDAI GROSSE.

ILLUMINATED BY THE LIGHTNING WAS THE GROTESQUE CORPSE OF THE MASTER OF THE ESTATE. AND YET...

IT'S TRUE THAT MY FAMILY WAS AS GOOD AS DESTROYED BY THE GROSSE FAMILY.
BUT REALLY.
I OWE A DEBT OF GRATITUDE TO THE MASTER.
(SERVANT) KOUGAIJI.
KOU...
(COOK) DOKUGAKUJI.
IF CRIMES WERE THAT SIMPLE, WE WOULDN'T NEED POLICE.
THE STORM RAGES ON AS THE NEXT DAY DAWNS...
THE EXISTENCE OF A YOUNG MAN CONCERNED WITH REBUILDING HIS FALLEN NOBLE FAMILY COMES TO LIGHT.
BRINGING WITH IT THE SECOND TRAGEDY OUTLINED IN THE "CURSE SUTRA."
MADAME!
THIS IS ALMOST UNDOUBTEDLY A SERIAL KILLING.
...IT'S MY TURN NEXT, I RECKON.
HEY.
THERE'S AN UNDERGROUND PASSAGE HERE!

A BLACK SHADOW DRAWS UP BEHIND GOJYO AS HE APPROACHES THE TRUTH.

WAIT A SECOND.
I'VE SEEN AN EARRING LIKE THIS BEFORE.

AND THE INTERMINGLED LOVE AND HATE BETWEEN THE RESIDENTS OF THE MANOR GRADUALLY BECOMES MORE COMPLEX.

THEY'RE ACTUALLY BROTHERS?!
LORD HAZEL AND LORD KOU-GAIJI?! WHY, THAT'S IMPOS-SIBLE!

IT'S TRUE THAT THE MADAME AND I HAD A PRETTY *DEEP* FRIENDSHIP.
BUT WHAT DOES THAT HAVE TO DO WITH ALL THIS?
WHAT IF...
...THIS IS ALL A TRAP, SET UP BY THE MUR-DERER?
THAT'S RIGHT-- I DID IT! I DID IT ALL!
GIVE IT A REST.
THIS IS A COMPLETE TRAVESTY.

HANG ON, SANZO!
YOU KNOW WHO DID IT?!
HN.
WHAT A PAIN IN THE ASS.
ANY SHIT-FOR-BRAINS CAN SEE THAT THE MURDERER IS *YOU.*
WHAT IS THE TRUTH THAT SANZO'S SIXTH SENSE LED HIM TO...?!
PREPARE FOR THE REVELATION OF THE TRAGEDY HIDDEN IN THE "CURSE SUTRA"!
STAY TUNED FOR THE SHOCKING CONCLUSION IN THE NEXT INSTALLMENT!
NOTE: PLEASE DON'T TAKE THIS SERIOUSLY.
THE END

最遊記
RELOAD

Coming soon in *Saiyuki Reload* vol. 9

koku is back and creepier than ever, and it's going to be the Maten
tra vs. the Muten if Sanzo has his way. Hazel's past is revealed, and an
citing showdown begins in the next volume of *Saiyuki Reload!*

SOUND EFFECT CHART

THE FOLLOWING IS A LIST OF THE SOUND EFFECTS USED IN *SAIYUKI*. EACH SOUND IS LABELED BY PAGE AND PANEL NUMBER, SEPARATED BY A PERIOD. THE FIRST DESCRIPTION (IN BOLD) IS THE PHONETIC READING OF THE JAPANESE, AND IS FOLLOWED BY THE EQUIVALENT ENGLISH SOUND OR A DESCRIPTION.

GIRI!

THIS USEFUL SOUND EFFECT HAS A COUPLE OF FUNCTIONS: IT CAN BE EITHER THE SOUND OF GRINDING TEETH OR TWO COMBATANTS STRUGGLING AGAINST EACH OTHER.

40 DO!X7: ENGINE RUMBLING
42.4 GASHA: CRASH
44.3 FUAAAAA: YAWN
45.1 DOSA: THUD
45.2 CHIKA: GLINT
46.5 BASA: FLAP
46.6 GYOU: SURPRISE
47.1 BA!: FLAP
50.5 DA!: DASH
51.1 BATAX3: RUNNING AWAY
55.2 DAX2: STOMP
55.3 FURA: SLUMP
55.4 GASHA: GRAB
55.5 BA: CLUNK
58.1 GARAX3: TRUNDLE
58.2 GUI: YANK
59.2 OO: HOWLING WIND
60.4 GATA: CLATTER
62.2 DOOON!: BOOM!
62.3 ZUZUN: GUNFIRE
63.2 ZUZUN: GUNFIRE
64.2 BEKI: CRACK
67.1 GAUN!X2: BANG!
67.4 DON: BAM
67.5 GASHA: KATCHK

11.4 ZAAH: WHISSH
13.2 GASHA!!: CRASH
13.3 GARA!X2: SLIDE
14.1 HYOI: LIFT
15.2 ZUN: BIG LIFT
15.3 SUTAX3: CLATTER
15.4 OOO: HUMMM
16.2 OO...: WOW...
16.5 DOSAA: KATHUD
22.5 BASAX2: FLAP
23.1 BA-!: BAM
24.6 ZAWA!: GRRR!
25.1 OOO: BAD ATMOSPHERE
33.2 DO!X4: ENGINE RUMBLING
33.5 SHORI-SHARI: SCRAPE-SCRAPE
33.6 SHORI-SHARI: SCRAPE-SCRAPE
34.1 ZAKU: SLICE
34.5 SHURI-SHURI: PEEL-PEEL
37.2 BIKU!: TWITCH
39.5 DO!X4: ENGINE RUMBLING
43.3 GASHAA!: CRASH!
44.1 GAU...N!: BANG!

DOKUN!

IN MOST MANGA, A PLEASANT LITTLE "DOKI DOKI" IS THE PREFERRED SOUND FOR HEART-BEATS, BUT IN *SAIYUKI*, THEY NEEDED TO KICK IT UP A NOTCH. "DOKUN" IS THE SOUND OF A PARTICULARLY STRONG HEART-BEAT, USUALLY RESERVED FOR MOMENTS OF EXTREME SHOCK OR DEMONIC TRANSFORMATION.

87.2	DOKA!!: SLAM
87.3	DAX2: BAM
88.3	HYUU: SWSH
89.1	DOSA: SLUMP
90.1	DOON!!: BOOM!!
93.1	GIGII: CREAK
94.2	DO!X2: RUMBLE
94.3	DO!: RUMBLE
94.4	DO!: RUMBLE
96.4	BURORORO0!!: ENGINE REV
99.1	GOOOO: ROARING FLAMES
99.4	GARA: CRUMBLE
101.2	OOH: ROAR
103.1	AAHNX2: WAAAH
105.2	HIHIIN!: NEIGH
105.3	GARAX2: TRUNDLE
106.1	GARAX2: TRUNDLE
106.2	GARA: TRUNDLE
106.5	DA!: DASH
107.1	GARA: TRUNDLE
107.2	GARAX2: TRUNDLE
107.3	GARAX2: TRUNDLE
107.4	DAN!: LEAP
108.1	GAA!: GRAB
108.2	GARAX4: TRUNDLE
108.3	GARAX2: TRUNDLE
108.4	GARAX3: TRUNDLE
108.5	GARA: TRUNDLE
108.6	GARAX2: TRUNDLE
113.3	ZUZAZAZAA!!: SKID HOP
114.1	GARAX2: TRUNDLE
115.1	GYURU!: SCREECH
115.2	KIKIN!: SKID
119.5	PII: FLICK
121.2	CHYARI...: TINKLE
121.4	POU...: MURMUR
121.5	GAA!: GRAB
122.4	BAKII!!: CRACK
123.1	ZAWA: SHOCK
123.3	ZUZUN: HUMM
127.4	BURORORO:ENGINE RUMBLING

ZAA!

YOU'LL SEE THIS ONE A LOT IN *SAIYUKI*. "ZAA" INDICATES A DRAMATIC APPEARANCE. IF YOU WANT TO MAKE A LASTING IMPRESSION, ALWAYS COME IN WITH A COOL POSE AND A BIG "ZAA!"

68.1	OOO: ROAR
68.2	DON!X3: BAM!
68.3	GAUN!!: BANG!!
68.4	ZAWA: GRRR...
68.5	FUOO: WHOOM
69.1	HYUU: SWSH
69.2	ZASHU: SLASH
69.3	BUSHU: RIP
70.3	DON!X2: BAM!
70.4	GUI: YANK
70.5	DA!: DASH
72.3	GIRI: CLENCH

ZAWA!

NO ONE REALLY CARES WHAT ALL THOSE EXTRAS IN THE BACKGROUND ARE SAYING, RIGHT? THAT'S WHY MANGA-KA USE THIS HANDY SOUND EFFECT TO INDICATE BACKGROUND CHATTER. YOU'LL SEE IT HOVERING OVER CROWDED CITY STREETS OR CLASSROOMS THROUGHOUT MANGA. IT CAN ALSO BE USED TO INDICATE THE SOUND OF WIND BLOWING THROUGH THE LEAVES OF A TREE. AIN'T THAT SWEET?

72.4	GAN!X2: WHAM!
73.1	BA!: SLAP!
73.3	DOOON!!: BOOM!!
74.3	GYU: TOSS
74.4	DOOON!!: BOOM!!
74.5	ZUZUN: GUNFIRE
78.1	ZUZUN: GUNFIRE
82.4	DA!!: DASH
82.5	BAAN!!: WHAM
83.1	BUWA: WHOOSH
83.2	GOOOO: ROARING FLAMES
84.1	OOH: ROAR
84.2	OH: ROAR
84.3	OH: ROAR
85.1	OH: ROAR
85.2	GAA!: GRAB
86.3	GIRI: CLENCH
86.5	JYAKA: KATCHK

158.4 BYUU: SWISH
158.5 BASHII!!: SLAM
159.1 GAN!: WHAM!
159.2 GASHAAN!: CRASH!
159.3 BUKUU: ZZZZZ
159.4 HYUNX2: ZOOM
161.2 FUOOO: HUUM
161.3 FUOOO: HUUM
163.1 HYUN: SWISH
163.3 KYUNN!!: WHIRL
164.1 GAKIIN: CLANG
164.3 BAA!!: GRAB
165.1 BYU...:ZZZ
165.2 DOGOO!:SMASH!
166.4 BISHII: THUMBS UP
173.1 KA!: FLASH
173.2 GOROX4: SQUISH
173.4 ZAAAAA...: (DRAMATIC ENTRANCE)
173.5 GIIII: CREAK
174.4 KYAAAA: EEEEEK!
175.1 KA!: FLASH
175.4 GATA:X2: GNAW
175.5 BYUOOO: HOWLING STORM
176.1 BONX2: DONG
176.4 ZAAAAA...: (DRAMATIC SCENE)
177.2 ZAWA!!: STARE
178.1 ZAWA...: MURMUR

128.1 DO!X3: RUMBLE
129.1 DON!: BOOM!
130.1 ZUZUUUN: HUUM
130.2 OOO: WIND BLOWING
133.3 DORUN!: BRUUN
136.1 DON!X2: BAM
136.3 GAUN!X2:BANG
137.1 GOH: KICK
137.4 TON!: TAP
137.5 DAN!: LEAP
138.2 TO!: TAP
138.3 BUAAAAH: HUUM

は っ
HAH!
THIS IS ONE OF THE MOST COMMON SOUNDS YOU'LL SEE IN MANGA. IT'S USED TO INDICATE SURPRISE AND IS USUALLY EQUIVALENT TO "GASP!" "H" ISN'T NECESSARILY VOCALIZED, THOUGH.

138.4 DON!: BOOM!
139.1 DOKA!!: SLAM
139.2 ZAA: (DRAMATIC POSE)
139.5 GACHAA: KATCHK
140.1 GAUN!: BANG
140.2 GAUN!: BANG
140.5 GA: CRR-
140.6 GO: CRACK!
141.4 DOON!!: BOOM
142.1 OOO: WIND WHOOSH
143.1 BA!: GRAB
143.2 DON!: BOOM
144.2 FUOO: HUUM
144.3 GYUN...: VVVV
144.4 PAAA!!: VVOOM
145.1 PIKU!: TWITCH
145.2 GARA: CRUMBLE
145.4 GAA!: YANK
148.4 BA!: WHP
148.5 GYAA: KAW
151.2 FUU: SIGH
156.2 ZUUUUUUN: IRRITATED
157.1 SUPAPAN!: SMACK SMACK
157.4 BASHI/BEKII!!: CLANK/CLUNK
158.1 GAKII!: BANG
158.2 ZAZAA: SSHSSH
158.3 DA!: DASH

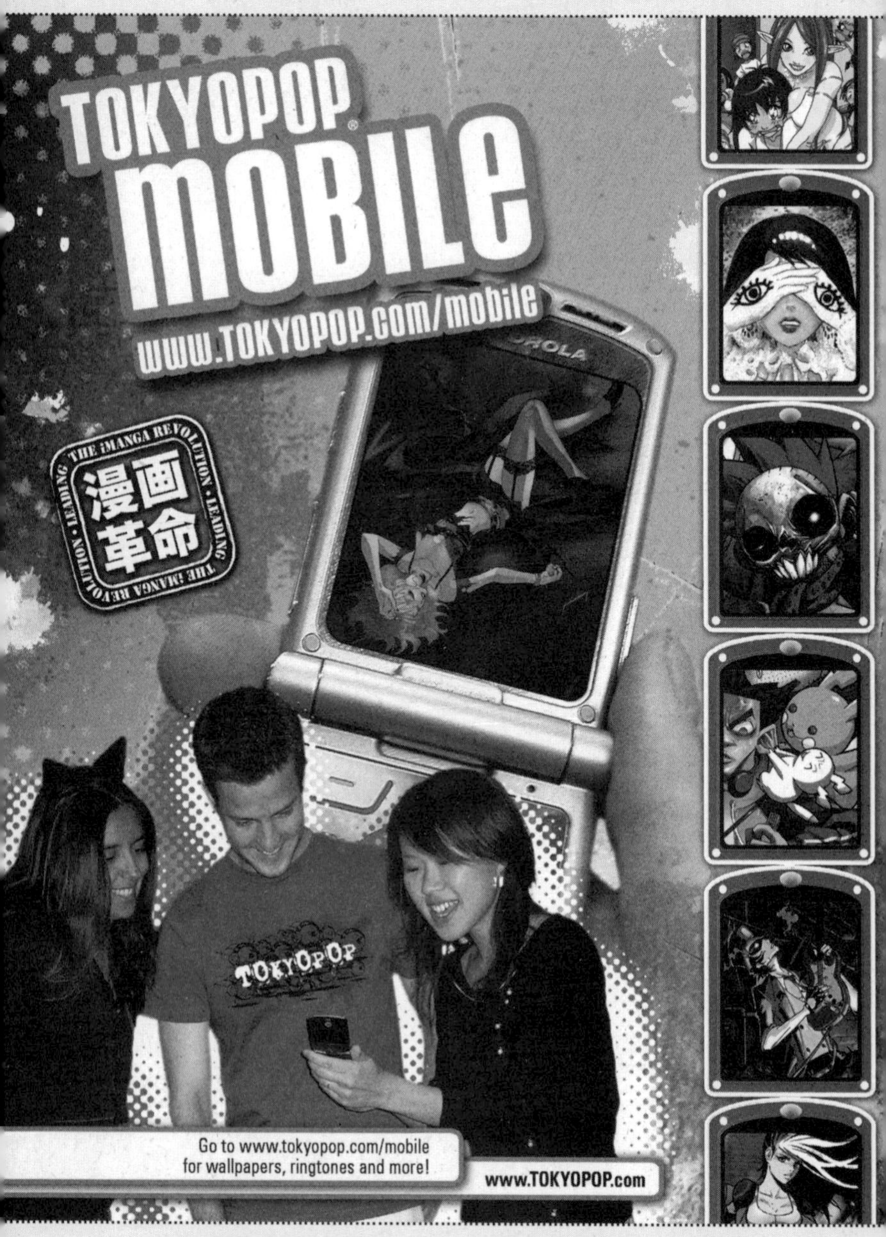

FOR MORE INFORMATION VISIT: WWW.TOKYOPOP.COM

Available at the iTunes Music Store and everywhere music downloads are available. Keyword: TOKYOPOP

New releases every month! Check out these great albums AVAILABLE NOW!!!

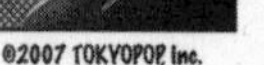

FOR MORE INFORMATION VISIT: WWW.TOKYOPOP.COM

Bizenghast™
The Bizenghast Novel Debut!
When a young Dinah moves to the forgotten town of Bizenghast, she uncovers a terrifying collection of lost souls. As she is forced to help these wandering spirits, one thing becomes painfully clear: The residents of Bizenghast are just *dying* to come home. This is an unforgettable Gothic drama that will leave you haunted long after the last page is turned.
Bizenghast
THE NOVEL
One
ART NOT FINAL
TOKYOPOP
Bizenghast
Check out the iManga at TOKYOPOP.com!
Bizenghast soundtrack available on iTunes
POP FICTION

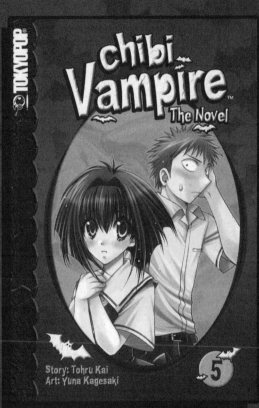

TOKYOPOP MANGA SUPPLEMENT

JYU-OH-SEI™

獣王星

DARE TO VISIT THE PLANET OF THE BEAST KING

Young twins Thor and Rai are kidnapped from their space station colony and dropped on the forsaken planet known to the universe as the Planet of the Beast King. Can they survive this harsh world infested with giant carnivorous plants and populated with criminal outcasts? And how will they be able to escape the planet when the only way off is to become the new Beast King?!

STOP!

This is the back of the book.
You wouldn't want to spoil a great ending!

his book is printed "manga-style," in the authentic Japanese right-to-left rmat. Since none of the artwork has been flipped or altered, readers et to experience the story just as the creator intended. You've been king for it, so TOKYOPOP® delivered: authentic, hot-off-the-press, d far more fun!

DIRECTIONS

If this is your first time reading manga-style, here's a quick guide to help you understand how it works.

It's easy... just start in the top right panel and follow the numbers. Have fun, and look for more 100% authentic manga from TOKYOPOP®!